How To Start An Online Business As Solo-E: Beginner Guide Step By Step

Foreword

Now you are in the digital era. You need to realize that in the current era there have been many changes, especially how you started your business.

Distance is no longer a problem. Internet network technology has brought you into a new world. Yupz offline business has shifted into an online business.

What does online business mean? What are the types of online businesses? how to succeed online business tips?

maybe you are hesitant to start an online business. Let me show you who are the 7 richest entrepreneurs in 2019.

You will be amazed how Jeff Bezos is the richest businessman in the world. What business does Jeff Bezos do? Do you know Amazon? Certainly!!

That is my rationale, how can we start an online business as Solo-E.

Solo-E is Solo Entrepreneurs which is an online business that is run alone even from home.

Come on, Have a book This will guide you as a beginner to be able to start an online business!!!.

Table of Content :

1. Understanding, Types, Benefits and Tips for Successful Online Businesses

2. How To Start An Online Business From Home

3. Top 7 Richest Entrepreneurs In 2019

4. How to Make a Free Blog to Make Money

5. How to Create an Online Store Website for Beginner Bloggers

6. 7 tools for online shop product optimization

Chapter 1

Understanding, Types, Benefits and Tips for Successful Online Businesses

Before starting an online business, it is good to follow the basic guidelines for business for the most complete beginners. This guide covers the understanding, types, benefits and tips for online business success in 2019. This is important in order to be able to find business opportunities in 2019.

Online businesses are booming since they entered the age of digitization. This condition triggered sending offline purchases for online purchases. It's no wonder that Internet marketers are becoming new professions for online business.

The interest plunges into an online business not just for small children, but the older generation does not want to be left behind. Finding an online business with promising small capital is an obstacle for beginners. Some even want to start an online business without capital.

The above conditions can be understood since the online business can be done at home. In other words, an online business is a business that can be done anywhere, including at home all day long.

So what do you recognize from an online business? It is a good idea to study online business from understanding online business, online business types, online business benefits, online business success tips and 2019 online business trends.

I'll share aspudin by writing the most complete online business guide for beginners.

What does online business mean?

The word online business is not new that we hear. So what is the meaning of online business?

Online business is the activity of buying and selling products made through the internet network. Therefore, the key word of an online business is the Internet network. Without it it's called an offline business.

In terms of online business, there are fundamental differences in how to sell offline and online. This will trigger different techniques and strategies of offline business marketing.

While understanding the online business according to experts is:

1. Yudi Wicaksono

Online business is to buy and sell activities in the internal connection and online shopping resources that are available.

2. Dedik Kurniawan

Online business is an activity that uses internet network facilities to carry out all activities such as business, lecture lists, search, pursuit, seeking news and so on.

Types of online businesses that are home-made

Happy unemployment is the term for online business people who work from home. They feel that they are actually free from time-regulated activities or from businesses with homes as a workplace.

Maybe you are confused, the kind of online business that can be done at home. Next, I offer the types of online businesses that can be done at home as follows:

1. Dropship

What is the meaning of dropship? Dropship is an intermediary that brings together suppliers and end users. As dropship, you do not come in direct contact with the product.

The activities carried out by dropshipper are promoting products for various online marketing goals. The best place to sell dropshipper online is e-commerce or the market.

The dropship market need not be confused to bring an audience. A dropshipper only focuses on selling.

The advantage of dropship is that there is almost no risk of loss unless you choose a supplier that is unreliable.

The lack of dropship is that the performance of the dropshipper is heavily influenced by the suppliers.

2. Freelance Writer

Freelance or freelance writers can be done at home. There are many websites that provide freelance writers like freelance, iwriter and so on.

Becoming a freelance writer requires the ability to write. A lot of reading is the key to being an online writer.

3. Ebook / Paperback / hardcover writers on amazon

To become an author of an Ebook / Paperback / Hardcover in Amazon Sagat is easy. There are no special requirements such as graduation from the school or work experience as a writer.

What it takes to become a writer and publisher of books on Amazon is to meet the applicable tax obligations. Do not worry, every book that sells well is taxed immediately. So the nominal you get is clean.

4. Blogger

Starting to become a blogger is not difficult and does not understand the programming language of the website. You just wrote an interesting article.

There are two major platforms that are often used by bloggers, bloggers and wordpress.

The income earned by a blogger comes from ads that appear on blogs and affiliate marketing.

5. Affiliate Marketing

Affiliate marketing is a type of online business that can be done at home. There are many Ecommerce that provide affiliate marketing.

All you need to do is promote Ecommerce products. The benefits obtained in the form of sales commissions.

6. Online shop

Online shop is a business that is done at home with a very broad market share. Online shops can sell products on their own website or in the marketplace.

How to make an easy online shop website can use the blogger platform.

The benefits of online businesses that are often felt

Starting an online business to succeed will provide many benefits. There are also benefits of online business as follows:

1. Free time

One of the benefits of online business is a lot of free time. If you already have a family, it will be very helpful to accompany your sons and daughters.

2. There is nothing to regulate

Running an online business that is done at home makes you nobody manage. That is because you are fully in control of the online business.

3. Creating jobs

The variety of types of online businesses can create new jobs. Of course it's good for people's welfare.

4. Reducing the flow of urbanization

Because online business can be done anywhere, it will automatically reduce the flow of urbanization. Wow it's really good so it's even distribution ...

There are many more benefits of online business that can be felt by the community.

Online Business Success Tips

Tips for successful running an online business can start from building your own character. Here are tips for successful online business:

1. Personal branding

Personal branding is forming one's own character. If you like sharing, your personal branding is like sharing.

2. Trust

Keep the trust that your clients give. If you don't get trust you can do it with the original name and address.

3. Costumer Review

Customer reviews will greatly help develop your online business profile.

4. Easy to contact

What's wrong today, what's wrong? Approximately so many questions arise in the minds of your clients. Try not to reply late to the conversation. Sometimes 30 minutes don't have a response, your clients will hesitate and even leave you.

How are you interested in running an online business that can be done at home?

Chapter 2

How To Start An Online Business From Home

An online business is a business that is done through the Internet network. Everyone can do it from home, but how can I do it? I know it's difficult, but I'll show you how to start an online business from home.

You know, the home is the best office to reach the money. It can be crazy. No, that is possible. The way to work from home is an online business. Therefore, the Internet network is a part of success.

For beginners, starting an online business that can be done at home without capital will be very confusing. This is because we do not know the type of online business that can be done at home without capital. Well, I'm going to show you the types of online businesses that can be done at home without capital.

An online business in which you have not worked seriously gives you the opportunity to succeed in the field of online business. Who is quick who can. This is what the saying says.

To grow an online business is not difficult enough to have an internet network. Your name is also an online business that needs an Internet network to connect between sellers and buyers.

Relax, there are many types of online businesses without capital that can even be done at home.

Maybe you can not wait to start an online business that is done at home without capital.

The following types of online businesses that are done at home without capital are:

1. Dropship

Dropship is a type of online business that can be done at home. Although it requires capital, there is almost no risk of loss.

The Dropship actors are known as dropshipper. A dropshipper can do business anywhere, including houses.

What a dropshipper should recognize is a reliable supplier. If you choose the wrong provider, it will disrupt your credibility.

2. Affiliate marketing

Affiliate marketing is a type of online business that lacks the capital to sell products. What you have to do is the promotion of the product.

Affiliate merchants are a term for people who are involved in Internet marketing.

The advantage is the sales commission.

Many e-commerce applications and markets offer affiliate marketing.

3. Author

Freelance writers can be a new business opportunity for those of you who want to try it out in 2019. The amount of new bloggers that appear and author services is an indicator to start an online business as a writer.

It is easy to become an online writer, the most important thing is to have a reading and writing hobby.

4. Blogger

Being a blogger is a good business opportunity in 2019. There are no specific conditions to start an online business as a blogger.

How to get money from bloggers is to monetize your blog or you can also open a template and SEO optimization services.

Google Adsense is an easy way to get money from bloggers.

5. Youtuber

Being a YouTube partner is a new online business in 2019. How to get money from YouTube is the monetization of the YouTube channel.

Google Adsense on YouTube is an easy way to get money from the YouTube channel.

6. Entrepreneurship Solo

The online business venture is to build a blog as an online media store.

The online sale is made with management and control in the hands of the owner. The wide reach makes the solitary enterprise an excellent online business.

7. The author and the editor are independent.

Being an independent writer and editor can be done at Amazon.

The way to get money at Amazon is through the production of e-books, paperbacks and hardcover books.

It's a small online business opportunity without capital that can be done at home in 2019.

When you try to start an online business, a classic problem arises, capital. How is it possible to run an online business without capital?

Chapter 3

Top 7 Richest Entrepreneurs In 2019

Entrepreneurs are people who start a business with a high financial risk. Do more than risk. That's what sets me apart from entrepreneurs.

When I started writing the 7 best entrepreneurs, you could guess why they were very familiar with your business. Perhaps one of the 7 richest entrepreneurs is your inspiration. That means you're on the right track.

It is very simple to know what your business is, but it is very difficult to succeed like them. You know it.

So who are the 7 richest entrepreneurs in 2019?

Let's check this out the top 7 most affluent wealthy business owners are (as forbes latest report):

1. Jeff Bezos

Jeff Bezos

Last year and now in 2019, Jeff Bezos is being the 1 richest businessman in the world. I have net worth of $ 112 billion. Top 1 businessmen.

Jeff Bezos is founder and CEO of Amazon. Amazon is the e-commerce giant.

Now amazon not only Ecommerce but also has diversified business interest like web service, alexa, audible etc.

You know, 1994, Jeff Bezos starts an online business with the bookstore. Now you can see what Jeff Bates has achieved. Top 1 Entrepreneur.

You know I'm very happy to be part of Amazon as Ebook Publisher.

2. Bill Gates

bill Gates

Bill Gates is number two on the list. Shareholders' equity of US $ 90 billion. Bill Gate is the founder of PC software company Microsoft Corporation. For the past two years, Bill Gates in second place after Jeff Bezos.

Bill Gates has been interested in computers and programming science since a very young age. At age 13, the father of three children first met computers when he bought the ASR Model 33 Teletype terminal and several General Electric (GE) computers for students. The downside of using a computer at this point is that it can not be used any longer. Bill Gates, Paul Allen and his friends decided to exploit a bug in the operating system to get more time to use the computer. Even as a teenager, Bill Gates and Allen's computer skills enabled them to accept multiple offers from various companies to write programs or applications. Gates used this opportunity to study various computer programming languages.

3. Warren Buffet

Warren Buffet

Warren Buffet owns Berkshire Hathaway.
Warren Buffet is the successful investor.
Shareholders' equity of US $ 84 billion.

The man born on 30th August 1930 has several companies, and the most important is Berkshire Hathaway. Buffett shows great interest in business and investment at a very young age.

4. Bernard Arnault

Bernard Arnault

Shareholders' equity of US $ 72 billion. Bernard Arnault is the President and CEO of the fashion conglomerate LVMH. LVMH is the largest luxury company in the world.

As an art patron and collector, he is the visionary behind the Louis Vuitton museum, designed by Frank Gehry for $ 135 million at the Bois de Boulogne in Paris, which opened in October 2014.

Mark Zuckerberg

Mark Zuckerberg

Shareholders' equity of US $ 71 billion. Mark Zuckerberg is founder and CEO of Facebook.

The initial inspiration for Facebook's creation may have come from the Phillips Exeter Academy, a private school where Zuckerberg graduated in 2002. He publishes his own student directory, a class of books that students call "Facebook."

6. Amâncio Ortega

Amâncio Ortega

Shareholders' equity of US $ 70 billion.

Amancio Ortega Gaona is the founder of the Inditex Group, a large company that controls the network of clothing and accessory stores in Zara. Through the company, this man born on March 28, 1936 managed to collect assets of $ 70 billion

7. Carlos Slim Helu

Carlos Slim Helu

Shareholders' equity of US $ 67 billion.

Carlos Slim Helu owns America Movil. America Movil is Mexico's largest mobile telecommunications company.

Once you know the list of the 7 biggest wealthiest entrepreneurs in 2019, you may feel that there are similarities in the business field you build.

Everything you need to do is consistent. Is very difficult.

Chapter 4
How to Make a Free Blog to Make Money

Tutorial on how to create a free blog about money-making bloggers. Maybe you are one of the people interested in creating a blog. Be listening to stories from friends or anyone who can make money from blogging. Well, I'll write to you about creating a free blog about bloggers who can make money.

The term for bloggers is the blogger. The term applies actively or not, as long as you have created a blog.

There are many purposes to create a blog, such as for an online store, selling SEO services or to make money.

For starters like me, the goal is to make money. If I am inspired by a success story of aspudin who can make money from blogging.

After reading the success stories of Indonesian bloggers who could make money from blogging, I started looking for ways to create a blog. It turns out that the way to do this is easy and even free.

In the past, I thought about creating a blog to take a course on how to create a blog. Again, my guess is wrong, to create a personal blog, it is not necessary to take private lessons to create a blog. It's easy to make a free personal blog. At where?.

To create a free personal blog may be in blogger or wordpress. I'm more interested in creating a free personal blog on the blogger.

While there are flaws if we create a free blog in blogger or wordpress, the domain we use is hosted by the owner.

If you create a free blog in blogger, the domain name will have a blogspot attachment. Whereas, if you create a free blog in wordpress, there will be a wordpress attachment. This is one of the disadvantages of creating a free personal blog.

It does not matter if creating a free blog can also make money from blogs. How do you make money from a blog?

Before answering the above question, of course we've done a blog first. So we just talked about making money from blogging.

Please note that this article specifically creates a blog on the blogger.

The following is how to create a free personal blog that can make money as follows:

1. Create a Gmail account

Please note that the blogger is owned by Google. Then we must have a Gmail account. In fact, using another email can also be used, but we recommend using a Gmail account.

If you do not have an email from Google, you'll need to create a Gmail account.

Creating a Gmail account is very easy. Just open it in the navigation and enter gmail. The next step is to fill out the form provided.

Once you have a Gmail account, you're ready to create a blog.

2. Open Blogger

Once you have a Gmail account, the next step is to open the blogger in the Google Chrome browser. Then you will be asked to sign in to create a blog. It's still easy so far, folks.

3. Create a blogger profile

The third step is that you will be prompted to create a blogger profile. There used to be two options for blogger profiles, that is, using Google Plus or the blogger's own profile.

Since Google Plus will close, you must create a blogger profile. You'll be prompted for a blogger's username and profile photo. My advice is to skip I change the profile photo of the blogger later.

4. Make a title, URL address and template

The next step is you will be asked to create a title, url address and choose a blogger template.

What you need to know is that creating a title must be unique so that it is easily detected by Google. It is usually best to choose the URL address of the blog URL.

Ur's address is never the same, so if you choose the URL address that is already available, it will usually have to change the URL address. Create a unique URL address, such as the URL name of this blog, which is calana bolong.

The URL selection of the blog URL should be the same as the blog title so that it is more user friendly. In fact, there is a good blog URL address tailored for the niche blog.

Blog niche is a common theme that will be discussed in blogs like SEO blogs, online businesses and so on.

Once you've determined the address and title of the blog, you'll be prompted to choose a blog template. Choose the best blogger template that best suits your taste.

5. Click on create a blog

The next step is to click on the blog, which means that your blog is ready to be used to post articles. So far, how to make a free blog is complete. But it still can not be indexed and appears in Google search.

How easy is it that guys do not create a blog? This method is an easy way to create a blog free blogger.

As the purpose of creating a blog is to make money, here I will briefly present the income settings.

If you pay attention on the blogger dashboard, there is no income. Now let's show income.

The following are displayed on the dashboard:

1. Open dashboard blogger

2. Click Settings

Setting blogger

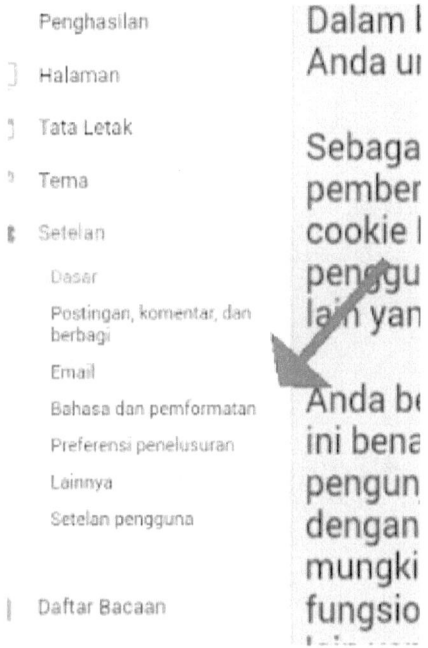

3. Click language

Suit blogger language

komentar Google+ tidak dapat di
tidak akan muncul lagi di blog An

Pelajari lebih lanjut.

Bahasa

Bahasa   Inggris (Amerika Serika

Aktifkan transliterasi ?   Dinonaktifkan ▼ pa

Format

Zona Waktu   (GMT+07:00) Jakarta

Format Header Tanggal ?   Monday, March 4, 2019

One of the conditions for displaying on blogger is American English.

4. Choose American English

5. Save

6. Reload the display will appear on the blogger dashboard.

Until here you already have a free personal blog that can make money from bloggers. But there are still conditions that bloggers must agree to in order to monetize the blog.

An easy way to make money from a blog is to become a google adsense publisher. Requirements accepted as a google adsense publisher are quality and useful articles.

If you want to make a blog it's finished and your article is ready. But there are still the next steps, namely how to optimize so that blogs are quickly indexed by Google.

You can find ways to optimize your blog in the next article.

For articles on how to make a free blog that generates money, it is enough.

Chapter 5

How to Create an Online Store Website for Beginner Bloggers

Are you looking for ways to create an online store site on blogger? If so, you read articles that are suitable for beginners. Here's a tutorial on how to create an online store website for bloggers for beginners.

How to make an online store website on blogger is different from other platforms like wordpress. If wordpress is a plugin, then the blogger requires the use of a script. Even so, how to create an online store website with the blogger can be considered relatively easy.

The digital age has driven the proliferation of online store companies. This opens up new opportunities to create an online store site. The goal of creating an online store website is to reach buyers outside the area. So how do you create an online store website?

Here's how to create an online store site with blogger, namely:

1. Go to the blogger

To create a blogger site is to open a blogger in google chrome.

2. Specify the profile name

Once you open the blogger, you will be asked to specify a blogger username. We recommend that you use the name that will be used for the domain name.

3. Site Title

The site title should be the same as the URL address that will be used.

4. URL address

The URL address is the domain name that will be used by the online store's site. The URL address should reflect which products will be sold on the website of the online store.

5. Model

The templates used should be those that support online store sites. Blogger has provided many template sites that are SEO friendly. But it is not suitable for models of online store sites. If you do not want a lot of tweaking templates, you should buy an online SEO model store.

6. Settings

Settings on the blogger dashboard include many things. Basic settings include the title, registered in blogger search or not, and include third-party URL settings. For online store sites, you must use third parties (Tld Domain). This is to facilitate the brand of the online store. Please purchase a domain from your domain provider provider.

7. Search Preferences

Open the blogger panel> settings> search preferences. Search preferences are intended to make online store sites easily found on Google searches. Write a description that explains the site as a whole.

8. Google Search Console

Dashboard> Settings> Google Search Console. Let the Google Search console click on it to be directed to Google Webmaster. In the Google webmaster dashboard, add the website address of the online store.

9. Check the website of the online store

To check the website of the online store, you can click on the URL address of the URL. Select the check. If you have already purchased a domain, it will usually be verified immediately, but for a larger property, you should check the html tag, the tag manager, and the tag analysis.

10. Sitemap

You can create sitemaps or sitemaps by clicking the domain name in the dashboard of the search console. If you use the old version search console, in the crawl section, click the sitemap. Then enter xml.

To the top, the online store website can start posting products sold. But it will look like a personal website. There is still the next way to make the website of an online store professional and convince buyers.

Chapter 6

7 tools for online shop product optimization

Let's start from the most basic question about online business. What is the purpose of content marketing? The purpose of content marketing is to increase sales volume on online stores.

Maybe you are still confused about where this article is going. So this way, from the point of view of the online shop owner, every online store owner would want to sell products every day. Whereas from the buyer's point of view, the buyer wants the product sought in accordance with his expectations.

As an online shop owner, you must realize that the first time attracting the attention of buyers is the product title and product image. For now, I will try to share tools for product optimization to sell every day using a free photo editor. Whereas how to make a title that increases sales will be discussed later in the day.

I know, not all online shop owners are used to using photoshop and graphic design tools. This is not a problem because there are many free online tools for product optimization.

1. Canva

Product optimization tools with a photo editor that I recommend is Canva. It's very easy to use Canva, just drag and edit several elements. The results of optimizing using

Canva will look amazing and you will look as if you are already adept at using Photoshop. I love it.

2. PlaceIt

It's amazing to see photo edits using PlaceIt. PlaceIt is different from other photo editors. You can do a lot of ideas on the photo you are going to edit like putting a smartphone in a table and more. Even the screenshot photos will be edited to be extraordinary. Cool

PlaceIt can also edit photos from an image url. Then you can do photo editing according to your imagination.

3. Death To The Stock Photo

It might be a bit like death to the stock photo. Actually the use is also rather complicated, you must subscribe to the email first, then you will get the photo that you expect.

4. Graphic River

Gravic River is intended for online stores using several banners. So, graphic river is the coolest banner maker tool. You will be able to easily create a product promotion banner.

5. Snagit

Maybe you are used to screens smartphone screens and you upload product photos. But it is often difficult to edit photos from the screenshots. Snagit is a tool to edit photos from screenshots. After screenshot, you can directly edit the photo. No need to save the results of the screenshot just edit photo.

The advantage of SnagIt tools is that we can easily add several text elements and others to the screenshoot before saving the image.

6. Lightshoot

Lightshoot is a photo editor tool from the screenshots. After completing the screenshot, we can directly edit the photo by adding text or crop.

7. IM Free

IM Free is a very good free photo provider. Cool photo collection that can be used in combination with other photos.

I think you have a favorite photo editor tool. Maybe the photo editor tools above can be a new reference for you.

Keep in mind, the first view is so tempting then it's up to the buyer. Make your product photo look very beautiful but still prioritize real photos.

www.ingramcontent.com/pod-product-compliance
Lightning Source LLC
Chambersburg PA
CBHW030516220526
45464CB00006B/2817